P9-CMX-662

On the Trail of

Lewis and Clark

A Journey up the Missouri River

Peter Lourie

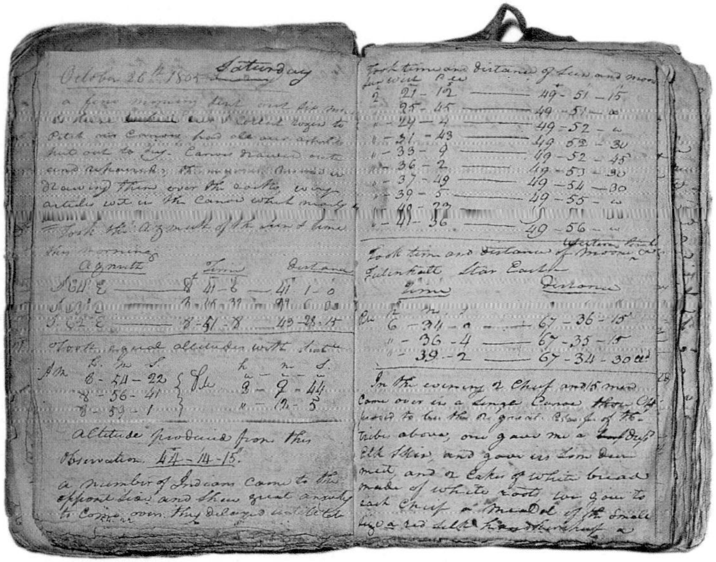

Boyds Mills Press

Additional photographs courtesy of:
Library of Congress: pp. 19, 22, bottom 23, 24 (painting by Karl Bodmar), p. 25 (photo by Edward Curtis), bottom p. 41 (photo by Edward Curtis); Bob Lindholm: p. 9; Missouri Historical Society: pp. 7, 29 left; Montana Historical Society: p. 20 (painting by Edgar Paxson); National Archives, Maps and Plans Group, Special Media Archives Division, College Park, Maryland: p. 6; Joslyn Art Museum, Omaha, Nebraska: p. 33; Nebraska State Historical Society, DeSoto National Wildlife Refuge: p. 13; Jerry Pospeshil: p. 14; U. S. Army Corps of Engineers: pp. 12, bottom 13.

Note: Traffic is prohibited on the Wild and Scenic section of the Missouri River for environmental purposes. The author and his companions traveled this section with the permission of the Bureau of Land Management.

Published by Boyds Mills Press, Inc.
A Highlights Company
815 Church Street
Honesdale, Pennsylvania 18431
Printed in China
Visit our website at: www.boydsmillspress.com

Publisher Cataloging-in-Publication Data

Lourie, Peter.
On the Trail of Lewis and Clark: a journey up the Missouri River / written and photographed by Peter Lourie. — 1st ed.
[48] p. : col. photos. ; cm.
Includes bibliographical references and index.
Summary: A present-day journey that follows Lewis and Clark's trail up the Missouri River.
ISBN 1-56397-936-5
1. Lewis and Clark National Historic Trail — Juvenile literature. 2. Missouri River — Juvenile literature. (1. Lewis and Clark National Historic Trail. 2. Missouri River.) I. Title.
917.804/ 33 21 2002 CIP
2001092181

First edition, 2002
The text of this book is set in 13-point Berkeley Book.

10 9 8 7 6 5 4 3 2 1

To Colin, Elena, Colleen, and Jim

—P.L.

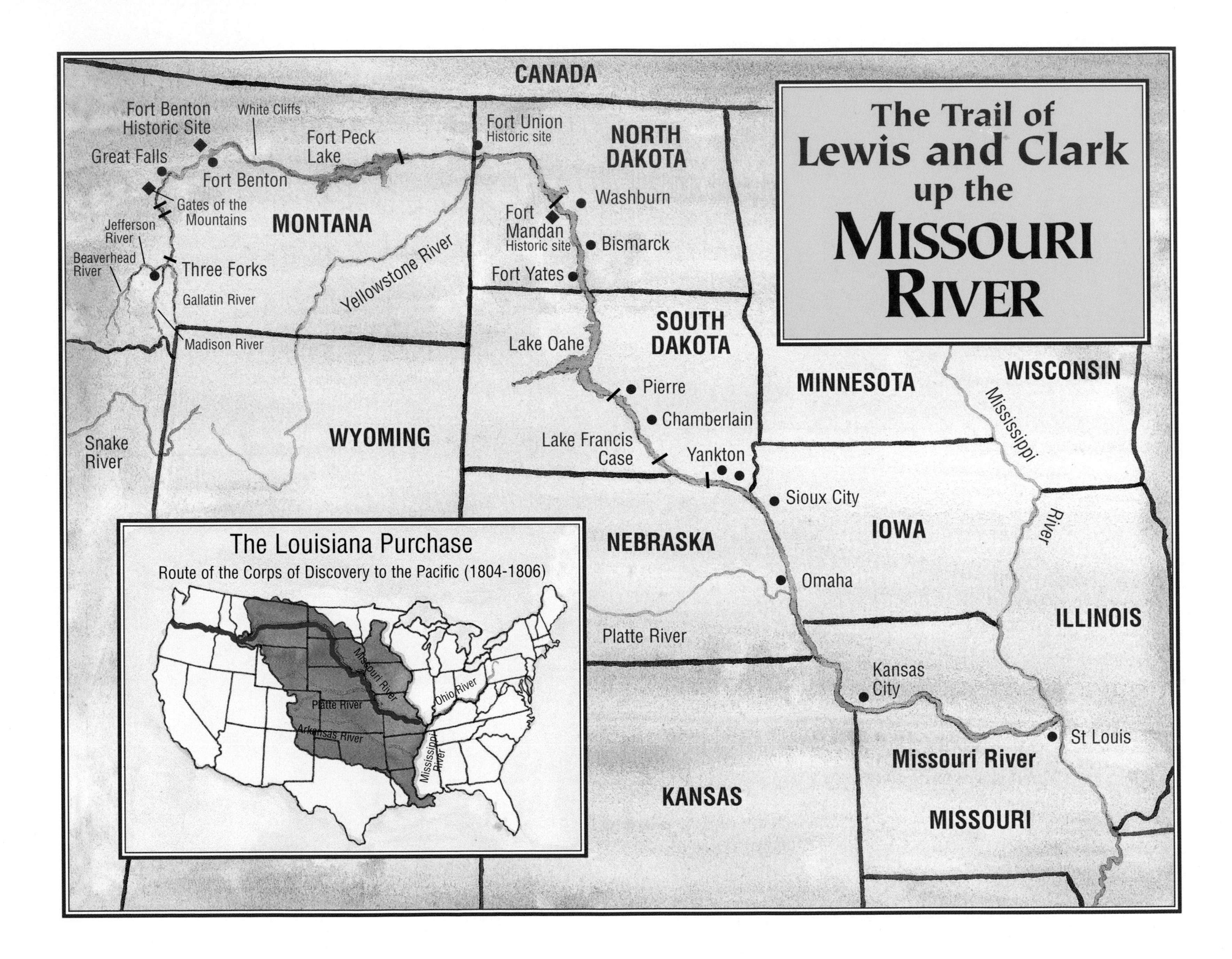

The Trail of
Lewis and Clark
up the
MISSOURI
RIVER
CANADA
Fort Benton
Historic Site
White Cliffs
Fort Peck
Lake
Great Falls
Fort Benton
Gates of the
Mountains
MONTANA
Jefferson
River
Beaverhead
River
Three Forks
Gallatin River
Madison River
Yellowstone River
Snake
River
WYOMING
Fort Union
Historic site
NORTH
DAKOTA
Washburn
Fort
Mandan
Historic site
Bismarck
Fort Yates
SOUTH
DAKOTA
Lake Oahe
Pierre
Chamberlain
Lake Francis
Case
Yankton
MINNESOTA
WISCONSIN
Mississippi
River
Sioux City
IOWA
NEBRASKA
Omaha
Platte River
ILLINOIS
Kansas
City
St Louis
Missouri River
KANSAS
MISSOURI
The Louisiana Purchase
Route of the Corps of Discovery to the Pacific (1804-1806)
Missouri River
Platte River
Arkansas River
Ohio River
Mississippi
River

Contents

A Map of Lewis and Clark's Track
Across the Western Portion of
NORTH AMERICA,
from the Mississippi to the Pacific Ocean,
By Order of the Executive of
The United States
in 1804, 5 & 6.
Copied by Samuel Lewis from the Original Drawing of Wm. Clark.
COLUMBIA
COLUMBIA RIVER
COLUMBIA VALLEY
Mt. Baker
Mt. Regniere
Mt. St. Helens
Mt. Jefferson
Clark's River
Lewis's River
Lewis & Clarks route
MISSOURI RIVER
LOUISIANA
Northern Boundary of Louisiana
A Band of Assiniboins 2000 Souls
Point of Observation
Black Foot Indians
Rocky Mountain
These Mountains are covered with Snow
Hot Springs
Travellers rest
FALLS
Marias R.
Medicine R.
Milk R.
Chilts 800 Souls
Chinnook 400 Souls
Cathlamah 300 Souls
Wahkiakume
Skilloot 2500 Souls
Clatsop 200 Souls
Chanwappan
Sok-kulk 3000 Souls
Wollaw-wol
Whe-el-po
Mick-suck-seal-tom Tribe 300 Souls
Hohilpo 600 Souls
Lax-ke-lo 900 Souls
Sketso-mish 2600 Souls
Tus-he-pah Nation
Shoshones or Snake Indians 2000 Souls
Shoshones 1800 Souls
Sho-sho-nes
Snake Indians
or about 10,000 Souls
Cal-lah-po-e-wah 3000 Souls
Mult-no-mah R.
South Fork of Lewis's R.
North Fork of Lewis's R.
Sholetts Lake
Flint Rock
Shush-pel-la-mine-mo R.
Yeppe Band of Snake Ind. 1000 Souls
Lake Riddle
Stinking Water R.
Boiling Spring
Salt Fork
Big Horn R.
Jefferson's R.
Madison's R.
Gallatin's R.
Philanthropy R.
Hot Spring
Colter's route in 1807
Cap. Clarks route
Clarks Fork
Yellow Stone
Ne-tusy 600 Souls Band of Snake Indians
Pa-kah 1000 Souls Band of Snake Ind.
Rio de San Clementine
Rio de la Plata
Highest Peak
Block House U.S. Factory in 1806
Rio de Nanesi
Arkansaw R.
RIO DEL NORTE R.
Cas-ta-ha-na Tribe 1500 Souls
Ki-a-wa Tribe
We-ta-pa-ha-to and Ki-a-wa 1800 Souls
Wisdom R.
Shoshones

PROLOGUE

Meriwether Lewis *William Clark*

The Missouri River is the longest river in the United States. If you measure its length from its highest pond source near Yellowstone Park, the Missouri is two hundred miles longer than the Mississippi.

For 2,540 miles, the Missouri cuts across seven states, running all the way from the Rocky Mountains in western Montana to its confluence with the Mississippi just north of St. Louis. It is also one of the most difficult rivers in the world to navigate and acts in swift, dangerous ways. Steamboat captains used to call the Missouri "Old Misery."

In 1803, France sold the Louisiana Territory to the United States. This was an 800,000-square-mile region west of the Mississippi River. President Thomas Jefferson purchased the land for fifteen million dollars, or three cents an acre. The Louisiana Purchase, as the act was called, doubled the size of the United States.

After acquiring the new land, President Jefferson commissioned Captains Meriwether Lewis and William Clark to explore the Missouri River and find the most direct water route to the Pacific Ocean for purposes of commerce and to observe the country, animals, and climate of the unknown land. He also wanted them to study the Indian nations along the way and to keep detailed journals about what they saw.

From 1804 to 1806 Lewis and Clark, along with a small band of adventurers called the Corps of Discovery, traveled by keelboat, canoe, and horseback from St. Louis, Missouri, to the Rocky Mountains, over the Continental Divide, all the way to the Pacific Ocean and back. In a little more than two years, they covered more than eight thousand miles. Much of that time was spent on Old Misery.

Nearly two hundred years later, I too traveled up the Missouri, along with three friends. For the big water we brought a twenty-two-foot-long, flat-bottomed boat with two Honda outboard engines; and for the shallower water we took a canoe with a small motor. Each one of us took turns driving the support vehicle, a Ford Bronco with a trailer at the back. Our goal was to follow the path of Lewis and Clark on the Missouri and to see just how much the river had changed since the days when the Corps of Discovery had traveled here.

A flooding Missouri River devastates a town.
Right: People try to hold back the water by building up the levees with sandbags.

Part One

Nebraska & Iowa

The Challenge

I started my Missouri River journey during one of the worst floods in a century. On the lower river, in Missouri and Kansas, people were desperately building up the man-made riverbanks, called levees, with sandbags. They were trying to keep the river from drowning their farms, their streets, their homes.

My friends and I put on our rain gear in Omaha, Nebraska, six hundred miles upstream from the river's mouth. We prepared for a long, cold, wet day. The wind was gusting to thirty-five miles an hour out of the northwest. Although it was June, it was only fifty-five degrees, rainy and misty, much more like autumn in New England.

The water was the color of milk chocolate, from all the earth it carried. The Sioux had called the river Mini Sose

Our own corps of discovery.

Unlike Lewis and Clark, we traveled in a twenty-two-foot-long fiberglass boat.

(Mi-ni So-say), meaning "muddy or roiled water." Big Muddy is another of the Missouri's many nicknames.

Lewis and Clark had set out with forty-five men. Our Missouri trip consisted of only four—Bill, Bob, Scott, and me.

We plowed into the swift current, but our boat was jolted back as if reeling from the punch of a giant boxing glove. For hours, we had to dodge whole cottonwood trees carried like torpedoes in the roiling, muddy water.

Keelboat

In the spring of 1804, the Corps of Discovery traveled up the Missouri with two small river boats and a fifty-five-foot-long boat called a keelboat. They poled, pulled, sailed, and rowed the keelboat, which held tons of cargo.

Twenty to forty men could pull the keelboat with a heavy rope, usually a thousand-foot-long line tied to the top of a thirty-foot-high mast. The long rope helped keep the boat away from shore. An average day against the current would take them only fourteen miles upriver.

The Great Plains Begin

Looking at the riverbanks, we noticed a change in topography. There was a touch of the Great Plains now in the land. From Kansas City north, the Missouri River forms a boundary between the eastern woodlands and the western prairie. Lewis and Clark had made note of the new landscape:

Moving into the prairie.

MONDAY, JULY 30, 1804

This prairie is covered with grass of 10 or 12 inches in height, soil of good quality. At the distance of about a mile still further back, the country rises about 80 or 90 feet higher, and is one continued plain as far as can be seen. The river meandering the open and beautiful plains. Catfish are caught in any part of the river. Turkeys, geese and a beaver killed and caught. Everything in prime order. Men in high spirits.

THE CHANNEL

In 1804, when Lewis and Clark moved up this lower part of the Missouri, the river was wide and shallow. It was also braided—made up of several channels that criss-crossed each other like strands of hair in a braid. The main course of the Missouri wandered across a wide, flat valley, called a flood plain.

But now people have pegged this part of the river down. The channel can no longer meander back and forth. On the lower Missouri, the U.S. Army Corps of

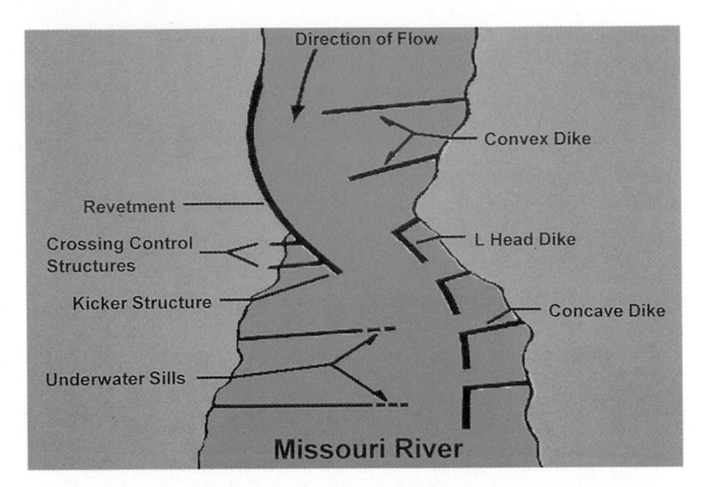

This chart shows the many underwater structures built by the U.S. Army Corps of Engineers to direct the flow of water on the lower river.

Parts of the upper river are still braided with sandbars and channels.

Engineers has increased the current by narrowing and deepening the channel. The Corps of Engineers is the branch of the U.S. Government in charge of maintaining commercial navigation on U.S. waterways. Over the years, the Corps of Engineers has straightened the Missouri River with the use of dikes and levees. Dikes are cement walls placed vertically in the bottom of the river to trap sediment. Levees are artificial banks that keep the river from moving from side to side.

During a flood (there have been at least six major floods since 1951), these levees sometimes cannot hold back the angry river. Like a trapped animal suddenly freed, the water tops the levees and spreads into the towns and farms.

The lower 732 miles of the Missouri, from Sioux City, Iowa, down to the Mississippi confluence, are called the channelized river. Here there are shipping lanes, buoys, and markers for boats to follow. By dredging, the Corps of Engineers maintains a shipping channel nineteen feet deep. The lower Missouri has been so altered by the engineers that it's almost impossible to know where the river of Lewis and Clark actually ran.

Steamboats

To avoid the dikes we stayed in the shipping channel. Willow and cottonwood trees lined the bank. Dark blue barn swallows, orange breasted with forked tails, flitted from shore. They sliced through the air, nearly touching the waves.

The Missouri has always been difficult to navigate. Good Missouri River pilots were in great demand. One steamboat captain wrote, "We used to separate the men from the boys at the mouth of the Missouri. The boys went up the Mississippi and the men went up the Missouri."

Between 1820 and 1890, more than four hundred steamboats sank or were stranded on the Missouri River. The 178-foot-long paddlewheeler *Bertrand* was one of the river's casualties. Designed to carry 250 to 400 tons of cargo, the *Bertrand* left Omaha on April 1, 1865, and hit a snag of tree trunks. It sank in twelve feet of water near DeSoto Bend on a part of the river that is no longer part of the river. The vessel was quickly swallowed by sediment. The river changed course over time and left the *Bertrand* in a field under thirty feet of silt and clay.

An artist's depiction of the Bertrand *sinking near DeSoto Bend.*

A work crew building a levee sometime around the turn of the last century.

Death of Sergeant Floyd

As we neared Sioux City, Iowa, we spotted the Sergeant Floyd monument ahead. The white monument rises high above the trees on the east bank. It is an obelisk, a hundred feet tall. The monument was built in honor of Sergeant Floyd, the only member of the Lewis and Clark expedition to die en route. He probably had appendicitis. Clark wrote:

The Sergeant Floyd Monument: a dramatic sight near the river.

Monday, August 20, 1804

Sergeant Floyd as bad as he can be, no pulse, and nothing will stay a moment in his stomach. . . . Sergeant Floyd died with a great deal of composure. Before his death he said to me, "I am going away. I want you to write me a letter." We buried him on the top of the bluff a half mile below a small river to which we gave his name.

For years, people came to visit Floyd's grave. But in the spring of 1857, when the river was high, part of the bluff was washed away. Floyd's bones were discovered sticking out of the cliff. So the people of Sioux City collected his remains and reburied them safely back from the river. Floyd's bones were dug up three more times and finally fixed in concrete at the bottom of the obelisk in 1900.

Bison

Lewis and Clark killed their first bison, or buffalo, near Ponca, Nebraska. Like musk ox of the arctic tundra, bison are an ancient animal that survived the ice ages in North America. Clark wrote in his journal:

Thursday, August 23, 1804

J. Fields sent out to hunt. Came to the boat and informed us that he had killed a buffalo in the plain ahead. Cap. Lewis took 12 men and had the buffalo

Buffalo like these in North Dakota once roamed the Great Plains by the millions.

brought to the boat in the next bend. Two elk swam the river, and were fired at from the boat. Several prairie wolves [coyotes] seen today. Saw elk standing on a sandbar.

Before the coming of white people, antelope, elk, bison, wolves, and grizzly bears were animals of the plains. As the prairie was settled, the big game retreated westward to the mountains. The bison were slaughtered—as many as sixty to eighty million of them!

Bill charts our course. Right: Prairie dogs, the "barking squirrels" described by Lewis and Clark.

PART TWO

SOUTH DAKOTA

Gavin's Point Dam, at Yankton, South Dakota: One of the many we had to go around.

YANKTON

In 1944, Congress passed a law to build six dams on the Missouri River for the purposes of navigation, irrigation, and the generation of power. The lakes formed by these dams line up for more than a thousand miles. Some call them the "Great Lakes of the Missouri." They have flooded thousands of acres of river valley and hidden many prehistoric and historic places. Indian villages, battle fields, fur trading posts, and hundreds of Lewis and Clark sites now lie underwater. The dam at Yankton, South Dakota, is the first of six major flood-control dams on the Missouri.

Yankton is a dusty town. The surrounding land is dry and flat. It was here the Corps first met up with the Sioux Indians. Contact with the Sioux was one of the expedition's main objectives, because the Sioux had all but closed the river to traders.

On August 29, 1804, Lewis and Clark met with five chiefs and seventy warriors of the Yankton Sioux. The Yankton Sioux were considered easier to approach than some other Sioux groups. Clark described them and observed many of their customs:

Thursday, August 30, 1804

The Sioux are a stout, bold-looking people, the young men handsome and well made. The greater part of them make use of bows and arrows. The warriors are very much decorated with paint, porcupine quills and feathers, large leggings and moccasins—all with buffalo robes of different colors. The squaws wore petticoats and a white buffalo robe with the black hair turned back over their necks and shoulders. In the evening the whole party danced until a late hour.

Lakes

We were entering ranch country, the high plains, the Missouri Plateau. On the plains of present-day South Dakota, Lewis saw three thousand buffalo in one viewing. Around Niobrara, Lewis and Clark saw their first prairie dogs, or, as they called them, "barking squirrels."

On Lake Francis Case, another huge reservoir, the wind was brisk out of the southwest, the chop moderate. We docked in Chamberlain, South Dakota, for the night. Here Lewis and Clark had seen an abundance of wildlife. They were the first whites to observe and write about the mule deer, the cutthroat trout, the western meadowlark, the grizzly bear, the pack rat, and the black-tailed prairie dog.

One thing is for sure, we were now on river time. Traveling all day in the hot glare of a river, we felt our

Lake Francis Case.

lives existed outside of normal time. Day after day, there was nothing but the waves and the wind and the open sky. It was easy to forget the world and its problems. Our daily task was simply to move ahead, always ahead. Lewis and Clark felt the same daily push, and in their journals they simply wrote, "We proceeded on."

THE TETON SIOUX

We came to Pierre, South Dakota. As Lewis and Clark approached the land of the Teton Sioux nearly two hundred years ago, they grew tense. They expected trouble from a people who had a reputation for demanding extravagant gifts from traders. Some called the Tetons "the pirates of the Missouri River." In order for the United States—the new owners of the immense Louisiana Territory—to establish control of the fur trade, President Jefferson needed to form good relations with the Tetons. This was the task set before Lewis and Clark.

Hundreds of Tetons gathered along the river. Their chiefs tried to bully Lewis and Clark. The Tetons could have massacred the explorers but did not, perhaps because of the bravery and determination shown by the explorers. At one time, the Teton warriors strung their bows and drew arrows from their quivers as if to shoot. Lewis then ordered his men to point their rifles at the chiefs. Suddenly, Black Buffalo, the grand chief, put a stop to the intimidation, and a fight was avoided.

Lewis in council with unknown Indians: This drawing was made by Patrick Gass, a member of the expedition.

On September 26, both Clark and Lewis were carried on white buffalo robes to the great council lodge in the Teton village. Buffalo meat roasted over fires. Speeches were made. The explorers were offered dog meat, a delicacy to the Tetons. Musicians played drums, shook rattles, and sang. Teton women danced, holding the scalps of slain enemies.

Today the Teton Sioux are the largest of the Sioux groups. The Teton family is divided into smaller bands, such as the Oglala, Brule, Miniconjou, and Hunkpapa.

Again fearing an attack at any time, Clark slept little. "I am very unwell for want of sleep," he wrote. Two days later the boats moved upriver once again. But Lewis and Clark had not fully accomplished Jefferson's goal of making a friendly impression on the Sioux.

PART THREE

NORTH DAKOTA

We explore a remote area of the river. Right: Native American children paddling on Lake Oahe.

Constructing Fort Mandan: This drawing was made by Patrick Gass, a member of the expedition.

LAKE OAHE

Just north of Pierre, we pulled around the huge Oahe Dam, the ninth largest dam in the world. We then set off on Lake Oahe, the biggest lake in the Missouri River system. Oahe stretches 231 miles from Pierre, the capital of South Dakota, to Bismarck, the capital of North Dakota.

Never before had the Missouri looked more like an ocean. For a long while we couldn't even see the shore. The sky and the water blended into one gray smudge. Lake Oahe has more than 2,250 miles of shoreline. We tied the bow and stern lines to bushes and climbed a hill. The wind blew hard across the prairie. How remote this place seemed.

Sitting Bull, the legendary Hunkpapa Sioux chief, in a photograph that bears his signature.

Standing Rock Indian Reservation

We pulled into a marina on the Standing Rock Indian Reservation. Nearby we spotted large white canvas tipis. A group of Sioux children had come for a weekend retreat to camp, swim, fish, and canoe.

It wasn't far from the marina that the great Hunkpapa Sioux chief Sitting Bull was born in 1831. He also died here on the Standing Rock Reservation. At fourteen, when Sitting Bull became a warrior, the first wagon trains filled with settlers were beginning to cross the Great Plains, headed for Oregon. When he was older, Sitting Bull watched the soldiers force Indians onto reservations. To protect the Black Hills, sacred to the Sioux, he was determined to fight. So he gathered many tribes: the Cheyenne, the Blackfeet, the Arapaho, and others. It was a fight for survival. On June 25, 1876, General George Custer decided to attack the Indians. Although he and his regiment had been commanded to wait until other troops arrived, Custer wanted to be the one to win against the great Sitting Bull. He thought he was attacking only a few hundred Indians. When he attacked the Hunkpapa camp, thousands of warriors counterattacked, and Custer's two hundred soldiers were annihilated within hours. The battle on the Little Bighorn was a major victory for the proud and determined Sioux and Cheyenne people, but it was to be their last. Exhaustion, starvation, and the superior military force of the white men drove the Sioux out of their sacred Black Hills and onto reservations.

Grave

In 1890, Sitting Bull was shot and killed on Standing Rock. The body of the Hunkpapa chief was placed without ceremony in a simple grave in Fort Yates, North Dakota. For sixty years his grave was neglected. Then on a dark, cold, and raw spring night in 1953, a group of his relatives dug up his remains and reburied them high on the bluff known as Standing Rock, overlooking Lake Oahe.

On the monument, I found his Indian name: "Tatanka Iyotake: Sitting Bull (1831–1890)." The location overlooking the Missouri River was so beautiful I felt moved to prayer. I prayed out loud into the wind that Sitting Bull did not die in vain. I prayed for Tatanka Iyotake and for his people. Then I went back to the boat, and we got underway.

A massive monument marks Sitting Bull's grave site.

Fort Mandan

Above Washburn, North Dakota, we passed near the place where Lewis and Clark spent their first winter, Fort Mandan. The actual site had washed away over the years.

On October 26, 1804, the Corps of Discovery reached the great earth lodges and villages of the Mandan and Hidatsa Indians at the confluence of the Knife and Missouri Rivers. Lewis found a good place nearby to build a fort for the winter. He and his men spent 138 days at Fort Mandan.

Sacagawea joined Lewis and Clark in what is now North Dakota and made a major contribution to the expedition.

The Bison Dance of the Mandan Indians.

On December 7, the river closed up with ice. Three days later, a herd of buffalo crossed over the river without breaking through. It was a tough winter. Temperatures dropped to forty-five degrees below zero. During the long winter wait, the men collected as much information as they could about the river to the north and west. Most of this information came from the Hidatsa Indians.

A French interpreter for the Hidatsa asked if the captains might need his services. His name was Charbonneau. One of his wives was a young Shoshone woman, only sixteen or seventeen years old. As a girl, she had been captured near the Rocky Mountains by a Hidatsa war party. Her name was Sacagawea, which means "Bird Woman" in the Hidatsa language.

Lewis and Clark hired Charbonneau, who planned to travel with his wife, Sacagawea. The captains realized that the girl might be useful to them when they reached the Rockies. She could speak to the Shoshone. Maybe she would convince her people to help the expedition, which needed horses to cross the big mountains.

On February 11, 1805, at Fort Mandan, Sacagawea gave birth to a boy, Jean Baptiste.

Into the Unknown

Although for thousands of years native people had traveled up the Missouri above the Knife River, few if any white people had done so. From here, up the river to the Rockies was uncharted territory for the Corps.

In late March, the river ice began to break up. Clark observed Indians skillfully jumping from one cake of ice to another "for the purpose of catching the buffalo as they float down." And on April 7, 1805, Lewis and Clark, along with the Corps and Sacagawea and her baby boy, finally left Fort Mandan to travel upriver into the great unknown. Lewis wrote:

A Mandan lifts a buffalo skull to the sky in this photo taken in 1908.

The reconstructed Fort Mandan.

FORT MANDAN, APRIL 7, 1805

This little fleet, although not quite so respectable as those of Columbus or Captain Cook, were still viewed by us with as much pleasure. We were now about to penetrate a country at least two thousand miles in width, on which the foot of civilized man had never trodden. I could but esteem this moment of my departure as among the most happy of my life.

Lewis reported lots of birds: whooping cranes, mallard ducks, meadowlarks, magpies, crows, bald eagles, great quantities of geese, hawks, and sharp-tailed grouse. He also reported in his journal how much he liked the taste of beaver meat, "particularly the tail and liver."

THE YELLOWSTONE

From Williston, North Dakota, the run up the Missouri to the Yellowstone River is only thirty miles. Cottonwoods ran downstream in the channel, half submerged and deadly. At the mouth of the Yellowstone River, we steered the big boat right along the mud line where the two great rivers meet. Just above the confluence, the Missouri was not yellow anymore but a lovely deep green.

FORT UNION

In 1805, Clark thought someone should build a trading post or fort at the confluence of the Missouri and the

Yellowstone Rivers. Eventually, it happened. In 1829, Fort Union became the most important fur-trading post on the upper Missouri.

A replica of the fort has been constructed on the foundations of the old structure. By walking through the fort, we were able to get a sense of what it must have been like more than 150 years ago. Next to the front gate on the river side of the fort is a little window hardly bigger than a foot square. Through this tiny opening, the Indians passed their furs. Mostly these would have been buffalo hides. But furs from other fur-bearing animals were traded, too, such as elk, deer, wolf, coyote, gray fox, red fox, grizzly bear, beaver, bighorn sheep, ermine, muskrat, and otter. Only the chiefs were allowed into the reception room to trade.

A few feet from Fort Union, we crossed over the border and into Montana.

A replica of Fort Union.

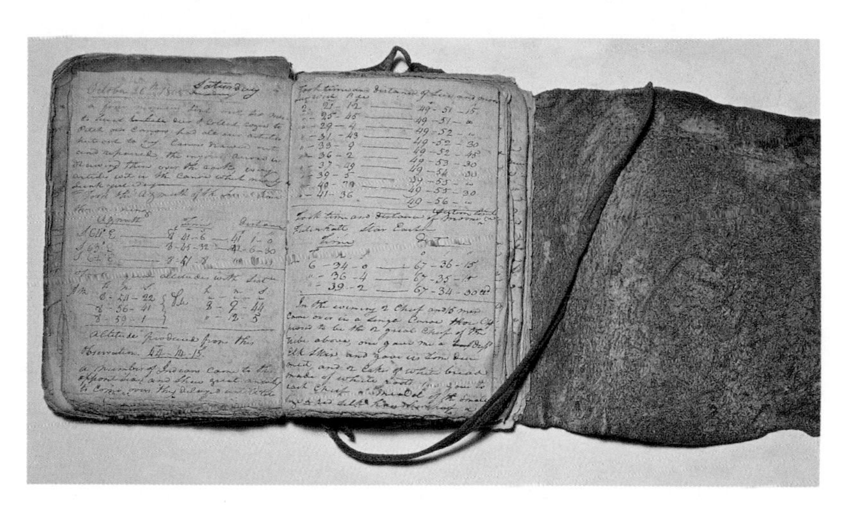

William Clark's elkskin-bound journal shows data he collected on October 26, 1805. Right: Bill and Scott on the long hot river.

Big country: Montana.

Part Four

EASTERN MONTANA

Stuck Again

Montana! All my life I'd wanted to visit this western state, the fourth largest in the union. Mountain lions, Rocky Mountain goats, elk, and bighorn sheep still roam here. In Lewis and Clark's day, Eastern Montana was grizzly bear country. Near Culbertson, the Corps had their first run-in with a grizzly—their first of many. Lewis wrote:

Monday, April 29, 1805

I walked on shore with one man. About 8 A.M. we fell in with two [grizzlies] . . . both of which we wounded; one of them made his escape, the other after my firing on him pursued me seventy or eighty yards, but fortunately had been so badly wounded that he was unable to pursue me so closely as to prevent my charging my gun. We again repeated our fire and killed him.

Fort Peck Indian Reservation

For four days now, we had labored on a sizzling hot section of the Missouri River with no mountains in sight. We finally came to the Fort Peck Indian Reservation, where we met Ken Ryan. Ken had been tribal chairman of the Assiniboin from 1984 to 1987. He told me there were four thousand Assiniboin here on the reservation and more than twenty-five thousand Assiniboin altogether in Montana and Canada.

Lewis and Clark had been very nervous as they passed through Assiniboin territory almost two hundred years ago. Lewis wrote:

Friday, May 10, 1805

We still believe ourselves in the country usually hunted by the Assiniboins, and as they are a vicious ill-disposed nation, we think it best to be on our guard.

"But we are not a fighting people," Ken told me. "My mom's great-great-grandfather was taken to Washington, D.C., in 1837 by President Andrew Jackson. He spent a year with the whites. When he came back, he told our

Ken Ryan.

tribe, 'We should never ever fight these white people. There are so many of them. They are like ants in an anthill. If we kill one, others will keep coming. There aren't enough Assiniboins to kill all the white people.' "

"I first swam in the river when I was four or five," Ken told me when I asked him about the Missouri. "To us the river is alive. We have a prayer about the Missouri River. When we see the river, we are taught to say, '*Mini-Shoshe*, Muddy Waters, it is good to see you.' When we leave the river, we say, 'Missouri River, *Mini-Shoshe*, Muddy Waters, I will see you again.' My grandpa taught me that if I said this every time I saw the river, I would never die in the river."

Fort Peck

When I looked at the Missouri the next morning, I made sure to say, "*Mini-Shoshe*, it is good to see you." But the sky darkened, and a big storm swept over us. Streaks of lightning blasted the sky. The thunder was like cannons firing in the west. The wind picked up in great gusts.

I pulled the canoe over to shore. Bill and I tried to get our raincoats on while hanging onto the canoe. The wind wanted to steal the boat from us. The waves bashed the shore, and now it was hailing and the hailstones hurt.

Five minutes later, magically, the storm had disappeared. The sky cleared, and the sun blazed as if there had never been a storm at all.

After nearly a week in eastern Montana, we were all tired of this kind of travel, and we craved the mountains. Lewis and Clark and their men were also tired of the long, hot days in this dry terrain. They, too, wanted desperately to see the Rockies. Lewis wrote:

Thursday, May 9, 1805

> *The river for several days has been as wide as it is generally near its mouth, though it is much shallower or I should begin to despair of ever reaching its source. . . . I begin to feel extremely anxious to get in view of the Rocky Mountains.*

Finally, we lifted the canoe on top of the Bronco and headed for the old Fort Peck Hotel.

Engine trouble.

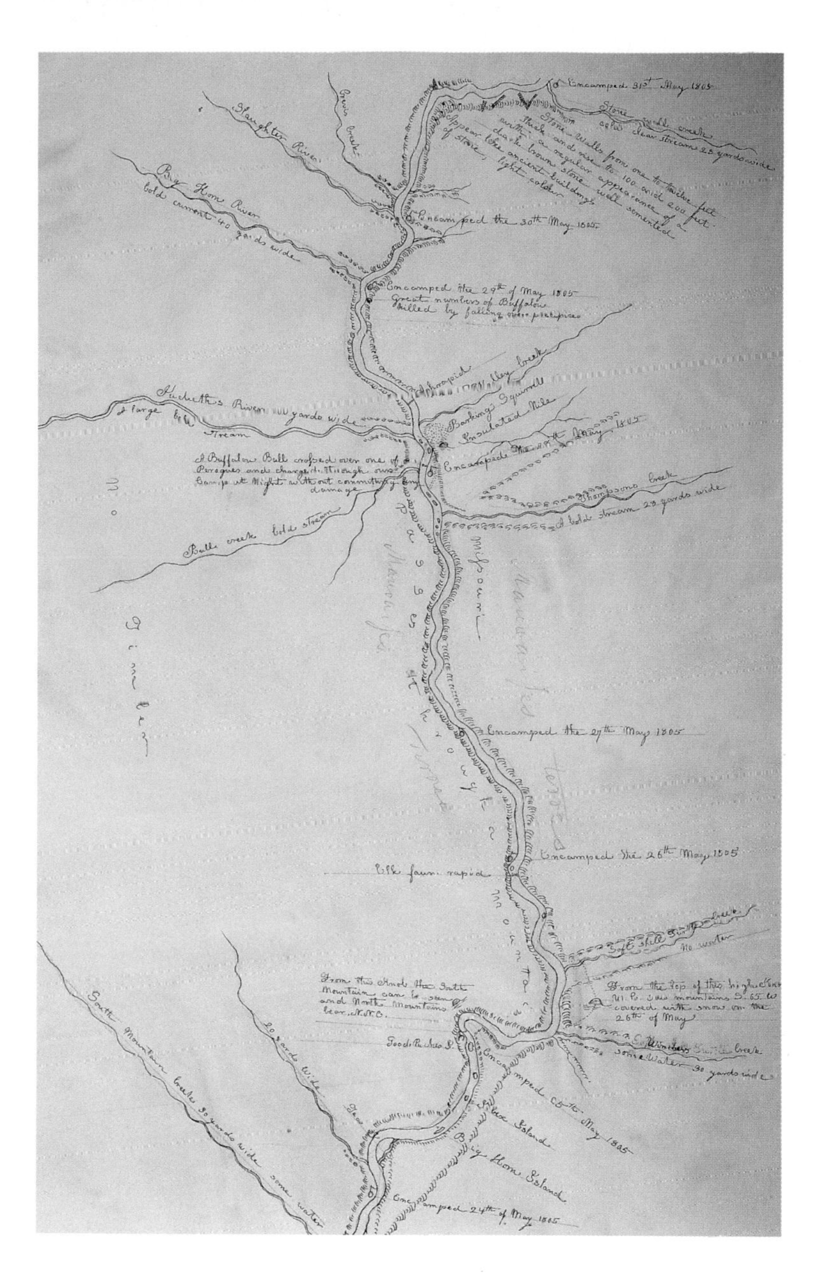

William Clark's map shows the White Cliffs region of the Missouri. Right: The Badlands.

Part Five

Montana's White Cliffs & the Rocky Mountains

The Badlands

Upstream from the Fred Robinson Bridge, a 149-mile-long segment of the Missouri has been designated a National Wild and Scenic River. It is protected and preserved in its natural, free-flowing state. It is almost the exact river that Lewis and Clark saw nearly two hundred years ago. We had been given permission to travel upstream in this section.

This part of the Missouri is managed by the U.S. Bureau of Land Management, called BLM for short. Chan Biggs of the BLM had been assigned to take us by jet boat to Fort Benton. In two days, we covered more miles than Lewis and Clark covered in twenty days of struggling upriver.

Chan was a cowboy in an official tan uniform. His hair was short and bristly, and he laughed heartily. "Jet boat"

The Corps of Discovery camped near this site.

sounds pretty fancy, but it was a regular flat-bottomed boat with a 115-horsepower Mercury outboard motor. However, this engine had no propeller. Instead, it pushed out a jet of air into the water, which drove the boat forward. The jet itself sits only a few inches underwater, allowing jet engines to travel in shallow sections where prop engines cannot go.

Pelicans scattered as we exploded upriver. We had now entered the so-called Badlands of the Missouri, named by the fur traders for the harshness of the region. Towering cliffs rose straight out of the water. Chan pointed out abandoned gold mines and homesteader cabins.

Even in the 1870s—the height of the steamboat era—there were few towns along this part of the river. This was Blackfeet territory, and the Blackfeet mistrusted intruders. The few towns that did exist were semilawless places, with justice by lynching. These hills had been havens for outlaws.

Chan pointed to the Corps's campsite of May 26, 1805. Here, Clark had climbed the bank of the river and spotted mountains to the west. He thought he was seeing the Rockies for the first time, but these were actually the Bears Paw Mountains.

White Cliffs

As we raced upriver, the land grew magical. The cliffs on both sides of the narrow river formed a kind of canyon. These were the White Cliffs of the Missouri.

Some of the formations had names like Dark Butte and Steamboat Rock. Steamboat Rock looked vaguely like a stone steamboat. High up, we noticed rock structures shaped like toadstools. Others resembled ancient walls. The whole scene grew stranger as the day passed.

Lewis said the rocks looked like the ruins of cities with massive buildings, spires, and statues:

Friday, May 31, 1805

The hills and river cliffs which we passed today exhibit a most romantic appearance. The bluffs of the river rise to the height of from 2 to 300 feet and in most places nearly perpendicular. They are formed by remarkable white sandstone. . . . The water in the course of time in descending from those hills and plains on either side of the river has trickled down the soft sand cliffs and worn it into a thousand grotesque figures. . . . As we passed on it seemed as if those scenes of visionary enchantment would never have an end.

Suddenly our engine coughed, then died. We floated quickly backward with the current. Chan tried the starter. Nothing. We drifted. "Well," he said, "guess we're out of fuel." He laughed halfheartedly. We had all hoped for a good dinner in Virgelle. But we were twenty-six miles away, and we had no food left in the boat.

Sheep Shed Coulee

At the side of the river in a place called Sheep Shed

The White Ciffs: As beautiful today as when Lewis first set eyes on them.

Stuck near Sheep Shed Coulee.

Evening settles on the river.

Coulee, we waited hours for help. Chan had been in touch over the radio with someone from his office in Fort Benton. The man tried to reach us, but the old road down to the river had been washed out long ago.

The last rays of the sun died on the cliffs across the river. The air grew cold. A meadowlark sang its lonely song, and the cliffs turned a roasted brown.

We decided to drift back five miles to a recently occupied homestead. Perhaps the rescue car could reach that place. Chan hung his head with fatigue. Bob, Bill, and I took turns with the paddles.

When we reached the homestead, Bill and I explored. It was eerie. The door was open. Bottles and cans still sat on the shelves. Finally the rescue car showed up. We refueled with difficulty in the darkness, and Chan decided to run the river in the dark, something no steamboat pilot would ever have done.

Wild Night Run

We raced toward the last glimmer of light in the western sky. For two freezing, dark hours we flew on a black river through a dark canyon of invisible rock. In the night sky the northern lights shimmered. The air was filled with the sharp smell of ponderosa pine.

At midnight, we were almost at Virgelle, and we could practically taste the food in our mouths. But Chan, having a hard time seeing the river because of the dial lights on the control panel, turned off the lights. He simply hit a button, and suddenly the motor went silent—hugely silent—and we began to drift once more. A fuse had blown!

Chan had no spare fuse aboard. So we paddled in the dark to shore. And now four cold, weary travelers began a long, long night hike.

Hike

We staggered up out of the river bottom and onto the high plains. We headed west, following the stars through a nightmare of barbed-wire fences and mud puddles. We passed through herds of nervous cattle, phantom shapes in starlight. For hours we stumbled onward, not knowing if we were anywhere near our goal. Distant lights twinkled and laughed at our folly. Then they disappeared altogether.

We began to lose all hope. At one point we dropped to the ground for a rest and immediately fell asleep. Chan roused us, and off we trudged. More cattle lowed in the darkness. More barbed-wire fences to climb. The night seemed truly endless.

Then, at four A.M., we spotted the river lights of Virgelle far below us, like a rescue ship at sea. We must have walked eight miles in four hours.

Virgelle is a town of only a few buildings, but there was food waiting, and soft beds. Next day, Chan got the motor going. We rode up to Fort Benton, one of the few larger river towns along the upper Missouri. Amazingly well preserved, this little town looks much today as it did

We were forced to paddle the jet boat to shore.

The Great Falls of the Missouri: Today the falls are controlled by Ryan Dam.

Prickly pear: The Corps found this plant a painful nuisance!

in the steamboat days. Front Street runs along the shore. Cottonwoods line the river.

Fort Benton saw its first steamboat in 1859. That's when the town became the head of navigation, meaning that it was the farthest point steamboats could travel on the Missouri. Above Fort Benton, a series of rapids and waterfalls blocked all river traffic.

Great Falls

Just upriver from Fort Benton, we came to Great Falls, Montana. The waterfalls here were an important landmark for the Corps. Back at Fort Mandan, the Hidatsa had told Lewis and Clark about the Great Falls of the Missouri. When the explorers found the falls, the Indians told them, they'd be close to the Rockies and on the right trail westward.

On June 11, 1805, Lewis and four men set out overland to find them. Clark proceeded upstream with the boats. On June 13, Lewis overlooked a beautiful plain, fifty or sixty miles wide. He saw more buffalo than he'd ever seen. Then he noticed something that gave him great pleasure.

Thursday, June 13, 1805

I had proceeded about two miles . . . when my ears were saluted with the agreeable sound of a fall of water. And advancing a little further I saw the spray arise above the plain like a column of smoke. . . . I soon [heard] a roaring too tremendous to be mistaken for any cause short of the Great Falls of the Missouri.

Portaging the falls with all their gear was extremely difficult. They built a wagon to carry the canoes. The wind was so strong, they hoisted a sail and actually "sailed" on dry land. The expedition spent a month portaging around the falls and preparing to move upriver. It was a horrible month. It was extremely hot. Prickly pear thorns penetrated their moccasins. The men limped and fainted. At night they fell asleep instantly, exhausted. Yet they remained cheerful and uncomplaining.

Jet Boat

The Missouri was now running so strongly, we weren't sure our little canoe could make it here. So we found a man named Jim in Great Falls, Montana, who was willing to run us up the river in his powerful jet boat. Jim's Thunder Jet could take us the ninety miles to Holter Dam in a few hours.

As we set off upriver, I spotted snow in the distant Bitterroot Range of the Rockies. Pine, balsam, and cedar trees grew at strange angles out of rock buttresses. The terrain turned rugged. This was definitely no longer the plains. Gone were the sandbars and the wide river. Gone were the bluffs. Gone was the muddy color of the water. The river had turned a dark green color. We were getting close to the river's source; I could feel it!

In Jim's jet boat, we covered a great distance in only a few hours.

For the next few days, Bill and I were back in the big boat on a series of reservoirs near Helena, the capital of Montana. We went out around Holter Dam, Hauser Dam, and Canyon Ferry Dam. These small dams were built for flood control, hydroelectric power, and irrigation. The lakes that formed behind the dams are used for recreation. It was a weekend, so we had to dodge water-skiers and fishermen.

Gates of the Mountains

The Missouri now squeezed through a rock canyon with thousand-foot-high cliffs on either side. I watched for signs of mountain goats in what Lewis called the Gates of the Mountains. The explorer found this terrain gloomy.

Near the Gates of the Mountains.

The Bitterroot Mountains.

He was desperate to make contact with the Shoshone Indians to get horses to cross the Rockies, but so far he had not met any Shoshone.

> **FRIDAY, JULY 19, 1805**
>
> *The mosquitoes are very troublesome to us as usual. . . . This evening we entered much the most remarkable cliffs that we have yet seen. These cliffs rise from the water's edge on either side perpendicularly to the height of 1200 feet. Every object here wears a dark and gloomy aspect. The towering and projecting rocks in many places seem ready to tumble on us. . . . I called it the gates of the mountains.*

The highest peaks of the Rockies now showed bright and snowcapped. We were getting very close to Three Forks, where three rivers come together to form the main stem of the river, and where I would end my seventeen hundred-mile-long Missouri River trip.

TOSTON DAM

My second-to-last day was one of the toughest river days of all. The mosquitoes were terrible, just as they were for Lewis and Clark. As usual, I was on the motor. We wanted to reach our final dam on the Missouri River, the Toston irrigation dam. We had only twenty miles to cover, but this distance took us close to nine hours. Our little motor could push the canoe a meager few miles per hour against the force of the current. The river was indeed raging.

As Lewis and Clark neared Three Forks, their spirits rose. Any moment they expected to meet the Shoshone. Lewis wrote:

MONDAY, JULY 22, 1805

The Indian woman [Sacagawea] recognizes the country and assures us that this is the river on which her relations live, and that the three forks are at no great distance. This piece of information has cheered the spirits of the party who now begin to console themselves with the anticipation of shortly seeing the head of the Missouri yet unknown to the civilized world.

We chugged up a small set of rapids and around a few big rocks. A storm was coming in. The smell of sagebrush was powerful. Thunder and wind blasted our backs. Bill moved suddenly to one side, and we nearly swamped. "Keep loose," I yelled at him. The boat was not making headway against the rush. I yelled, "Paddle!" But just then the little motor drove us slowly up and around a truck-sized boulder. Lightning all around now. Sky dark as night. Rain pelting us. On we pushed, right to the dam.

THREE FORKS

My last day on the river, I decided to travel downstream, the way of the current. We woke to gray skies and a blustery cold, like fall in New England—just like the day I had begun my trip way back in Omaha, Nebraska.

We drove to Headwaters State Park, where the

Toston Dam.

This photograph of a Shoshone man named Heebe-Tee-Tse was taken almost a hundred years after Lewis and Clark's encounter with the Shoshone.

Three Forks: Bill points to a digram of the Missouri headwaters in Headwaters State Park.

Madison and the Jefferson Rivers join to become the Missouri proper (the Gallatin enters just downstream). This is the very place that Clark stood on July 25, 1805. Although geographically the Missouri begins farther up—many miles up the Jefferson and the Beaverhead at the Red Rock Lakes—symbolically Three Forks is the beginning of the river.

Lewis wrote: *"The beds of all these streams are formed of smooth pebble and gravel, and their waters perfectly transparent; in short they are three noble streams."*

We began the day without the motor, paddling fast downstream. We swept past the Gallatin, the third of the three rivers. A contrary wind slowed us down, so we put away our paddles and started the motor. A large cliff jutted into the river. I was taking a photograph when suddenly the boat began to founder. Before I knew what was really happening, we were dangerously close to the edge of a whirlpool the size of a small building. I yelled to Bill, "Gun it!" Bill, who had not yet seen the whirlpool, fired the engine into full throttle, and luckily we inched our way up and out of that swirling boat-eater. Afterward, Bill said, "I didn't even see that thing!"

We raced downstream at fifteen miles an hour. White pelicans floated like kites against the gray cliffs. The majestic birds of the upper Missouri reminded me of how free I had felt during my five weeks on this incredibly difficult but beautiful river.

So much has happened in the two centuries since

Lewis and Clark first came here. Much of the wildlife has retreated to the mountains. The giant herds of buffalo are gone. Native Americans, who once roamed this big country, have been penned into relatively small patches of it. Many parts of the great river have been dammed, pegged down, and manipulated. And yet there is still wildness here, too, a great power only partially tamed.

We flew around a bend and came in sight of the Toston Dam. Suddenly the wind kicked up whitecaps and blew away the clouds. The canoe bounced hard against the waves. We spotted a bald eagle in the trees. The sky turned blue. And here was the sun, blazing on a hundred white pelicans as they whirled over our heads to say farewell.

White pelicans: As our journey came to an end, we caught site of these beautiful birds.

An abandoned homestead on the upper Missouri.

MO 9799 EX

EPILOGUE

Lewis and Clark finally did make contact with the Shoshone after they left the Missouri and headed up over the Continental Divide. Sacagawea was indeed helpful in getting her people to give the explorers horses to get over the mountains. After leaving the Missouri, the Corps went down the Snake, and Columbia Rivers to the Pacific, and finally reached the ocean on November 10, 1805. Clark wrote, "*Ocean in view. O. The Joy*."

The expedition spent its second winter, a wet dreary winter, on the coast at Fort Clatsop, in what is now Oregon. Then in March 1805, the Corps of Discovery started their long journey home to St. Louis. When they were all done, they had traveled an amazing eight thousand miles in nearly two and a half years. In so doing, they had described times and places and peoples that would never again be the same.

So much of their wonderful trip had taken place on the Missouri. In following their path up the river, I'd learned that much has changed in two hundred years, but the river remains hauntingly beautiful.

Mini-Shoshe, I will see you again.

Author's Note

• Including Lewis and Clark, there were thirty-three permanent members comprising the Corps of Discovery. Others joined for various periods of time, mostly at the beginning of the journey. Only thirty-three made it all the way up the Missouri, over the mountains, to the coast, and then back to the Mississippi. Lewis's dog, a Newfoundland named Seaman, completed the trip, too.

• Punctuation, spelling, and grammar in the journal entries have been edited and to some degree modernized for clarity. But I encourage the reader to go to the journals themselves to get a flavor for Lewis's and Clark's styles of writing.

• Traveling the Missouri River has taught me that rivers are like the veins of history. The story of our country can be studied along the watercourses of our nation's rivers. The Missouri, our nation's longest river, is perhaps the most historic, or, you might say, prehistoric. For thousands of years, various tribes moved up and down its massive current. Then came emissaries of a new nation, Lewis and Clark, and, after them, a wave of settlers from the East. For a brief period the Missouri was a major highway of steamboat and railroad travel, and then it was almost forgotten as we turned to automobiles and superhighways. Many of our country's rivers were abandoned.

Although the great Missouri no longer follows its original watercourse, and although it has been altered sometimes unrecognizably by human intervention, it nevertheless remains a wild river. To travel its path today is like traveling back in time, to a period long ago. Rivers like the Missouri have become places to rediscover, filled with raw beauty and many adventures.

Suggested Reading

To learn more about the Missouri River of Lewis and Clark, it is best to read the journal entries themselves. To picture what the river looks like today, some travel guides and photography books that cover the entire Lewis and Clark expedition may help. A few of the books listed here are for older readers, but younger readers can learn much from the photographs and maps in these books. For my taste, one of the best books about the Missouri that captures the real flavor of the river is *The River and I*, by John Neihardt, author of *Black Elk Speaks*.

Ambrose, Stephen E. ; Abell, Sam (photographer). *"Lewis and Clark: Voyage of Discovery."* Washington, D.C.: National Geographic Society, 1998.

Blumberg, Rhoda. *"The Incredible Journey of Lewis and Clark."* New York: Morrow/Avon, 1995.

DeVoto, Bernard, ed. *"The Journals of Lewis and Clark."* New York: Houghton Mifflin Company, 1997.

Duncan, Dayton. *"Lewis & Clark: An Illustrated History."* New York : Knopf, 1997.

Lourie, Peter. *"On the Trail of Sacagawea."* Honesdale, PA: Boyds Mills Press, 2001.

Neihardt, John G. *"The River and I."* Lincoln, Nebraska: University of Nebraska Press, 1997.

Schmidt, Thomas. *"National Geographic's Guide to the Lewis & Clark Trail."* Washington, D.C.: National Geographic Society, 1998.

White, Alana J. *"Sacagawea: Westward with Lewis and Clark."* Berkeley Heights, N.J.: Enslow Publishers, Inc., 1997.

Index